GILL

The TREASURE *in the* MUD

Illustrated by

Martin Cottam

OXFORD
UNIVERSITY PRESS

OXFORD
UNIVERSITY PRESS

Great Clarendon Street, Oxford OX2 6DP

Oxford University Press is a department of the University of Oxford.
It furthers the University's objective of excellence in research, scholarship,
and education by publishing worldwide in

Oxford New York
Auckland Bangkok Buenos Aires Cape Town
Chennai Dar es Salaam Delhi Hong Kong Istanbul Karachi
Kolkata Kuala Lumpur Madrid Melbourne Mexico City Mumbai Nairobi
São Paulo Shanghai Taipei Tokyo Toronto

Oxford is a trade mark of Oxford University Press
in the UK and in certain other countries

First published 2001

British Library Cataloguing in Publication Data
Data available

ISBN 0 19 915957 2

10 9 8 7 6 5 4 3

Printed in the UK by goodmanbaylis

Available in packs

Year 5/ Primary 6 Pack of Six (one of each book) ISBN 0 19 915963 7

Year 5 / Primary 6 Class Pack (six of each book) ISBN 0 19 915964 5

Contents

COTTAM
WHARF
A.PRIOR &

1
Cold Mud

"Charlie!"

Charlie lay still, on the floor, and kept his eyes tight shut. But it was no use pretending to be asleep. His mother leaned over the side of her bed, reaching towards him. Hooking her stick under the pile of old coats that he used as bedclothes, she flicked them aside and prodded at him.

"Charlie! The tide's almost on the turn. I can smell it. Get yourself down to the river, before it's too late."

Not yet! Surely it wasn't time yet!

Charlie grunted and rolled away from her. But the floor was hard and cold without his covers and there was nowhere to escape from that stick. His mother reached across the room and jabbed at him again.

"The others have gone down already. I heard that Joshua, out in the court. You'll miss all the best pickings."

Charlie was right up against the wall now. It was damp and mouldy, with a smell like river mud. He groaned, imagining how the cold, clammy mud would ooze up round his toes. He hated it when low tide was this early.

"*Up!*" his mother growled.

Charlie looked at her stick. Slowly, he hauled himself to his feet. "Let's have a bit of a warm first, Ma."

His mother almost screamed at him. "What are you going to use for coals? There's none here. Get down to the river and find some."

Charlie looked at the cold, empty

hearth and tried to think of another excuse. "Well, couldn't I just...?"

The stick prodded again, catching him in the back. "Get on with it, you lazy lump! And don't take that brown coat with you. It's... too good... for mudlarking..."

His mother fell back against her grimy pillow, gasping for breath. Then she started to cough. It was fierce, raw coughing that shook her whole skinny body.

Charlie gave in. "All right, Ma, don't take on. I'm going. Got anything to eat?"

She couldn't speak for coughing, so he rummaged in the basket beside her and found the end of a loaf. Pushing half of it into his mouth, he dropped the rest in her lap. Then he grabbed his mudlarking bag and ran out of the room.

It was three flights of stairs down to the courtyard. As he went down, he passed a dozen doors, with a different family

behind every door. Each room had its own particular smell of old cabbage or dust, stale meat or dirty clothes. On the landings, the different smells met and mingled, twisting their way down the stairs and out into the courtyard.

And that was where they stayed – trapped by the tall buildings all round. The courtyard was close and stuffy and it smelt terrible. It was still pitch dark down there. It took a long time for the daylight to get into Ironmongers Court.

But though it was dark, it wasn't quiet. There were always people awake in Ironmongers. As Charlie crossed the courtyard, he heard Liza's voice coming down from her window, two floors up. She was scolding her brothers and sisters.

" ... give over, do, or you'll wake Dad, and there'll be such a walloping... "

Then Peg came pattering down the stairs on the other side. She was always up early, to get to the flower market in time. She grinned cheekily at Charlie, swinging her basket.

"Why are you loafing around? You'll cop it if your Ma sees you. Joshua left an hour ago, with all his gang. There won't be a thing left by the time you get to the river."

Charlie pulled a face at her and tossed a stone towards her basket. But she skipped sideways, chuckling. Before he could catch her, she was through the arch and into the street.

Still annoyed, Charlie picked up another stone. For a second he weighed it in his hand. Then he threw it up at Alfred's window. That made him feel better. Why should Alfred, the schoolboy, lie snug in his bed when the rest of them were up and working?

* * *

Peg was right about Joshua. He and his gang were down by the river all right. The moment Charlie got near, he could hear them splashing through the low water, starting and stopping as they searched. The mud squelched under their feet and the air was full of its cold, rotting smell. Beyond them, the oily, stinking river shrank down the estuary and out to sea.

Charlie watched the boys for a moment or two, trying to pick out Flash Joshua. Normally that was easy. He had a big cord jacket, like a man's, and fancy curls arranged across his forehead. There were other mudlarks who tried to copy him, but none of them had the right threatening swagger. Joshua was the leader and he made it obvious.

This morning it was too dark to see the jacket or the curls. In the shadows, all the mudlarks were blurred shapes, hunched forward as they shuffled through the water, with sacks on their backs. But one of them was Joshua – and Charlie didn't want to be anywhere near him.

That meant working the bad patch, up against the Steps. The water there was too deep to search properly, even at low tide. But if he looked there, he might be able to hang on to anything he did find. As long as Joshua didn't notice.

Sitting down on a stone, Charlie rolled his ragged trousers up as far as they would go. The stone was cold – almost as cold as the river would be – but he couldn't afford to notice that. He had to get into the water, while there was still time. Soon the tide

would sweep back up the river and cover the mud for another twelve hours.

Charlie padded down the slimy Steps and slithered left, away from the other boys. None of them spoke to him, but their heads lifted for a second. They glanced round, working out who he was.

Ignoring them, Charlie squelched around the Steps, moving slowly. Wriggling his bare toes into the soft river bed. The black water came over his ankles

and his movements stirred up the mud, releasing bubbles of stinking gas. He took another step, and another, feeling the way with his toes. He was hunting for lumps in the mud.

It was amazing what landed up there. All kinds of things were dropped off barges or washed down the river. Books and braces and bits of ivory. Cast-iron saucepans and pieces of pottery. Candle-snuffers and pairs of spectacles. The mudlarks never knew what was going to catch against their feet.

Just now, Charlie was hoping to find some coals. Coals to burn at home and copper nails and bones to sell. Those were always easy to get rid of.

Slide and wriggle and slide. Every time he felt something hard he bent to fish it out. If it was anything good, he dropped it into his bag. Then on he went. Slide and wriggle and slide. The cold crept up his legs and the mud stuck to his arms, but he couldn't stop. Not yet. Slide and wriggle and slide...

After half an hour, he had found seven bones, a bit of dirty rope, and a couple of pieces of coal. He knew there wouldn't be much more. The river was glinting in the early light and the rising water was already above his knees. Joshua and the others were starting to move towards the Steps, with bags and baskets bulging.

Charlie started to panic. He couldn't stop yet. He hadn't found enough.

Desperately, he shuffled sideways, digging his toes in harder – and something sharp stuck into his foot.

"Oww!"

He couldn't help it. He knew it was stupid to make a noise like that. The moment Joshua heard the noise, he stopped and turned round to see what was happening. But Charlie couldn't keep the sound back. His foot hurt. Whatever he had trodden on was very sharp. Much sharper than a nail.

Standing on one leg, he lifted the injured

foot out of the water. The sharp thing came with it, dangling painfully. Leaning over, Charlie tugged it out and rinsed it in the black water. Then he bent to look at it.

It was a brooch. But what a brooch! It was as big as the palm of his hand, heavy and golden, with bright, glinting stones. He'd never seen anything like it. Not close to, at any rate.

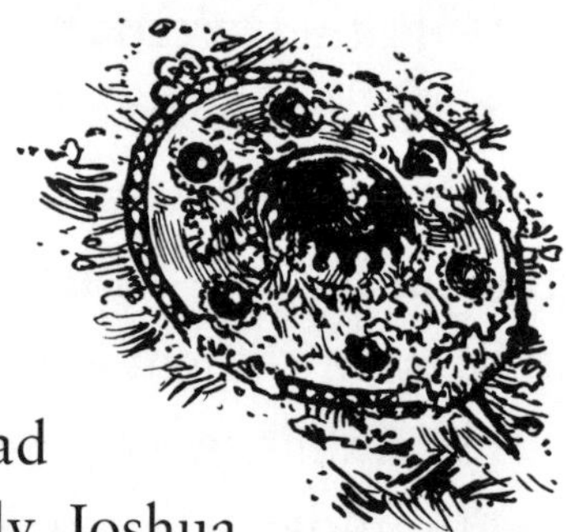

"Swipe me!"

He muttered the words, before he could stop himself. That was a really bad mistake. Immediately, Joshua ran down the Steps and back into the water. He began to splash towards Charlie, moving as fast as he could. The rest of his gang followed, as though he'd given an order.

"What've you got, young Charlie?" Joshua shouted. "Give us a squint."

Another minute, and he would have lost

it! Charlie knew exactly what they were going to do. It had happened a million times before. Joshua would grab him and push his arm up behind his back. Then the others would arrive, and duck him under the filthy water. They would hold him there, until he opened his fingers and gave up the brooch.

Well, they weren't going to get it! Quick as a flash, scrabbling and slipping in the slime, Charlie lurched to the next set of steps and hauled himself up. The moment he was on the bank, he started to run.

He didn't waste any time looking over his shoulder. He knew exactly what was happening behind him, because he could hear Joshua shouting to the others.

"Spread out! I'll stay on his tail so we know where he's gone! You go round the other way and cut him off!"

Bare feet pounding, breath coming in huge, tearing gasps, Charlie headed away from the river, doubling round corners and

ducking along back alleys. For a moment he thought he'd done it, that there was no one chasing him after all. Maybe Joshua had given up.

Then, way behind, he heard the sound of thudding footsteps, and he knew that he was wrong. Joshua hadn't given up at all.

He'd stopped to pull on his boots.

That was another reason to keep running. They were cruel, heavy boots and Joshua wasn't squeamish about kicking people. Gulping another mouthful of air, Charlie ran on, pushing himself to go even faster.

Heading for Ironmongers.

2

Hot Water

"Liza! LIZA! For Gawd's sake – "

Charlie pounded on the door with his fist, clutching the brooch in his other hand. His lungs were bursting and he could feel the blood thumping round his body. Liza had to let him in! It was no use going home. His mother wouldn't be any use against Joshua, but Liza might be able to help him. She always had good ideas…

"LIZA!"

When the door opened, he fell over, into the room. There was never much space in there, and he landed on top of Billy and Joe and little Sairey-Ann. Billy shouted and punched him and Joe began to wail. Sairey-Ann just giggled into his ear. It took a lot to stop her laughing.

Liza was by the fire. She was holding the baby under her arm and stirring some boiling washing with a stick. The whole room was full of steam.

"Cut that out, Billy," she said sharply. She looked down at Charlie. "You in a hurry?"

Sairey-Ann giggled again – and so did someone else. Charlie peered through the steam and saw Peg sitting on the window sill.

She grinned at him. "What's up? Stolen the Crown Jewels, have you?" Her lap was full of flowers from the market. She tied up one little bunch and began on another. "Are the bobbies chasing you?"

Charlie scrambled up and slammed the door shut.

“No bobbies,” he said. “Worse than that. Joshua’s after me.”

“Joshua?” Peg dropped the bundled flowers into her basket and slid off the sill. “What have you been up to?”

Charlie didn’t try to explain. He just held out his right hand and opened the fingers, one by one. Even through the steam, the brooch shone at them with the dull, solid glint of gold. Joe's mouth fell open and Billy stared.

"So help me!" whispered Peg. "It *is* the Crown Jewels."

Liza peered at it, and then looked sharply at Charlie. "Where'd you get that? Have you been nicking stuff again?"

"No, I never! Honest, Liza, I never!" Charlie shook his head fiercely. He hadn't forgotten the roasting she gave him when he stole that coat. "I didn't nick it – I found it. Just now, in the river. Down beside the Steps. What do you reckon it's worth?"

"I–"

But before Liza could get another word out, Billy gave a yell.

"Joshua's coming! He's coming! I just seen him run into the court!"

He pointed at the window, jumping up and down with excitement. Joe started to wail again, clutching at Liza's skirt.

Billy looked scornful. "You're a baby,

Joe! I'm not going to cry! I'm going to hit Joshua and thump him and punch him and…"

"No you're not!" Liza said stoutly. "You're going to stay out of his way! That Joshua–"

She didn't finish, because they all heard Joshua's feet, thudding on the stairs. He knew well enough where Charlie would have run to and he was making straight for the room where they were.

"Don't let him have the brooch!" Peg said. "Quick!"

She grabbed it out of Charlie's hand and threw it towards the big pot hanging over the fire. Her aim was perfect. The brooch sailed across the room and fell, with barely a sound, into the boiling, soapy water.

She was just in time. A second later, a heavy foot thudded against the door. The latch gave way and the door swung open.

"Got you!" Joshua said smugly. "I knew you'd be here."

There was complete silence. Joe clung on to Liza, too terrified to cry. Sairey-Ann had stopped smiling and she was staring at Joshua with big, wide eyes. Even Billy looked scared.

Joshua grinned. “Right then, Charlie. Let’s have it.”

Charlie tried to look innocent. “Have what? What are you on about, Josh?’

One corner of Joshua’s mouth twisted into a jeering smile. “Don’t come that with me. You found something in the mud, didn't you? I heard you yelp. What was it? Where've you put it?"

"Didn't yelp for nothing," Charlie said. "Only an ugly great nail that stuck in my foot."

Joshua didn't bother to argue. He pushed forward, sweeping the little ones out of his way, and grabbed Charlie roughly. Holding him by one arm and the seat of his trousers, he turned him upside down, shaking hard.

"Leave it out, you bully!" Peg thumped at Joshua with both fists. "Let him alone! Whatever he found, it's none of your business."

"That's right!" yelled Liza. "Get yourself out of here, Flash Joshua, or I'll send for my Dad."

Tucking the baby more firmly under her arm, she snatched up the stick she had been using to stir the washing. Joshua just ignored her. He didn't take any notice, even when she started to hit him with the stick. He was busy looking for a pocket in Charlie's ragged shirt and trousers.

There wasn't one to find. The clothes hardly covered Charlie as it was. There was nowhere left to hide anything.

Joshua was furious. He threw Charlie to the ground and stormed round the room, pulling the covers off the mattress in the corner and wrenching open the door of the little cupboard where Liza kept the plates.

"Here, you! Lay off!" Liza walloped him across the shoulders with the washing stick. She must have hit him very hard, because the stick snapped, with a loud crack. One end flew sideways, only just missing Joe's head.

The shock of it was too much for Joe. He sat down on the floor and gave a loud howl. "The stick's broken! It's bro-o-o-ken! How can we get things out of the water?"

"SSSH!" said Billy fiercely.

Too fiercely. Joshua looked sharply at him. Then, slowly, he turned towards the fire. There was a gleam in his eyes.

"Don't be daft!" snapped Liza. "That's boiling, that is. You let it alone."

Joshua ignored her. In two quick steps, he had crossed the room. Grabbing Liza's shawl off a chair, he wound it round his hands, to protect them from the heat. Then he pulled the big black pot off its hook over the fire and dropped it on to the floor, tipping it forward.

Steam billowed out and hot, soapy water flooded across the floor boards. No one had any time to think about the brooch. Liza held the baby high and snatched up Sairey-Ann with her other hand. Charlie heaved Joe off the floor. Peg grabbed Billy and lifted him on to the window sill. And all the time, the three of them were dancing from foot to foot, trying to keep out of the boiling water themselves.

Joshua was the only one who didn't care. He had thick boots on and he could ignore the water. With one boot, he pushed the wet clothes around the floor, peering down at them through the steam.

"You let that be, Joshua Vardy!" Peg panted fiercely. "Folks' clean washing is none of your business. You can't... OUCH!"

She yelped and jumped back as the hot water swirled against her toes. Joshua was kicking at the washing, separating the garments with his feet.

He kicked again – and suddenly there it was. The brooch. It looked even brighter now.

Even Joshua stopped for an instant. He looked down goggle-eyed, staring at the circle of gold with its glittering coloured stones. But he wasn't still for long. Before anyone else could move, he bent and scooped up the brooch, with an ugly grin at Charlie.

"Must be my lucky day," he leered.

Then he was gone, pounding down the stairs with hard, heavy feet.

Liza ran to the door and yelled after him. "Bad luck to you! I hope the bobbies catch you with it!"

"We're not done yet!" Peg said hotly. "We can go after him!"

"Yeah!" said Billy. "Go after him!" But he didn't sound quite sure about it, even though he clenched his fists.

"What's the use of that?" Charlie said miserably. He stared through the window, watching for Joshua to come out at the bottom of the stairs.

But it wasn't Joshua he saw. It was Alfred. He was halfway across the court, with his school books under his arm.

"Hey! Alfred!" Charlie leaned out of the window, shouting and waving his arms. "Joshua's coming down. You've got to stop him!"

Slowly – maddeningly slowly – Alfred turned. He took a couple of steps towards them, gazing round to see where the voice had come from.

"ALFRED!" Charlie bellowed.

Beaming good naturedly, Alfred took another step forward. But his face was still blank.

"HEY! LISTEN!"

As Charlie yelled again, Joshua came racing out of the doorway at the bottom of the staircase. He looked up at Charlie, with a gloating smile – and bumped straight into Alfred. Both of them went flying.

"That's our chance!" Peg shrieked. "Come on! Let's get him!"

She rattled down the stairs, with Liza close behind her, still clutching the baby. Billy followed them, yelling at Joshua – but staying safely behind Liza. Joe and Sairey-Ann stayed at the top of the stairs, holding hands.

Charlie waited by the window, just for a second. He saw Joshua hit the ground, so hard that his clenched right fist slammed against the cobbles. His fingers opened and the brooch slid away, out of reach. Charlie could see it clearly, even from two floors up.

The brooch hit the edge of the open gutter in the middle of the court. Tipping over, it rolled a little way, and then slid through one of the holes in the grating.

Into the drain.

3
Down the Drain

Charlie raced down the stairs and out into the courtyard, with Joe and Sairey-Ann pattering behind him, still hand in hand. The others had reached Joshua already, before he had a chance to get up. They had thrown themselves at him and he was buried under a heap of bodies.

Peg was sitting on his chest, grinning triumphantly down at his face. As Charlie came up, Joshua stirred and tried to get up, and she pushed him down again.

"Keep still!" she said. "Or I'll tickle you

to death!"

Joshua groaned and fell back. Liza was on his legs, with the baby on her lap and Billy was sitting on his feet, bouncing up and down and scowling fiercely. Joshua looked furious, but he couldn't make a sound. Peg had stuffed a piece of old rag into his mouth.

Alfred was gazing down at them all, looking completely bewildered.

"It went into the drain!" Charlie said. "Did you see it? The brooch went down the drain!" He ran over to the grating and bent over it, peering into the darkness.

Joe and Sairey-Ann trailed after him. Joe tried to stick his hand through the grating, but it wouldn't go through, even though it was small. Charlie looked at Sairey-Ann, but she pulled a face and backed away, shaking her head so hard that the curls bobbed round her fat little cheeks.

"How about this?" said Alfred. He

pulled a ruler out of his school bag and passed it to Charlie. "That'll go in between the bars."

Charlie slid the ruler through the grating and poked around in the mud at the bottom of the drain. "That might be it. That shiny thing in the corner."

Alfred bent lower, trying to see. "It's a circle, isn't it? We could pull it out if we had a hook. On the end of a stick."

"Here!" said Peg. She put a hand up to her bonnet and pulled out one of the hairpins that held it on. "Bend this into a hook."

"But that'll spoil it," Charlie said.

Peg waved her hand grandly. "Get that brooch back, and you can buy me a real hatpin!"

"Thanks." Charlie grinned and bent the hairpin round one of his fingers, to make a rough hook. "Anyone got a bit of thread?"

Liza laughed and pointed. "There's a bit hanging off Joshua's shirt."

Ignoring Joshua's furious, purple face, she broke off the hanging thread and handed it to Charlie. He grabbed a penholder from Alfred's school bag and tied the bent hairpin to the end, winding the cotton round until the joint was firm.

"Now!" he murmured.

But he was too nervous. He knew that he had to hurry, to get the brooch before any of Joshua's friends appeared. And he kept thinking about how valuable it was. Worth hundreds of pounds. *Thousands.* He couldn't bear the idea that they might turn up and snatch it away from him.

The more he thought about that, the more his hand shook.

In the end, Alfred pulled the penholder away from him. "You're not doing any good. Let me try."

He lay down on his stomach on the cobbles, to keep his shadow away from the grating. Very slowly, he slid the hook and the penholder down towards the surface of

the mud.

People were beginning to come down into the court, crowding close and asking questions.

"Lost something, then?"

"What's up with young Joshua?"

"Some kind of game, is it?"

Alfred ignored all the questions. Slowly and steadily, he edged the hook towards the brooch, aiming to fix it into one of the loops round the edge.

Peg glanced round at the curious, sharp-eyed crowd. Then she leaned closer to Charlie, to whisper in his ear. "You'll need to cut and run when you get it. Unless you want to answer a lot of questions."

Charlie nodded and wriggled nearer to Alfred, ready to grab the brooch as soon as he could.

Slowly, carefully, a hair's breadth at a time, Alfred slid the hook towards the brooch. The prong of the hook slipped neatly into the loop and the brooch lifted upright, on to its edge.

At that moment, Liza gave a loud, sharp gasp.

"Shut your noise!" Charlie hissed. "You'll put him off."

"But – look!"

Everyone except Alfred glanced towards the entrance of the court, and one of the watchers sniggered loudly.

"You lot are going to catch it now!"

Five of the biggest boys from Joshua's gang were swaggering into the court, shoulder to shoulder. The moment they saw what was happening, they began to run.

"That's Charlie!"

"And they've got Josh!"

Charlie's eyes flicked back to the drain. Quite calmly, undisturbed by all the noise, Alfred was just hauling the brooch up between the bars of the grating.

Charlie's hand flashed out like lightning. He grabbed the brooch off the hook and leaped to his feet, all in one movement. Then he was off, aiming at the narrow back alley that led through to the next court.

His feet were still sore from his last run, and he was panting before he had gone a hundred yards. But he could hear a terrible, angry bellowing behind him and he knew that he dared not stop.

The gang had got Joshua free. That made six of them to chase him. It was worse than last time, down by the river.

This time they knew what Charlie had in his hand. They weren't going to give up.

Charlie raced across the second court, glancing over his shoulder for an instant. It seemed as though the whole world was after him. Joshua and his friends were only a couple of seconds behind him. Then came Peg and Liza and Alfred, with the little children to slow them down. And after them was a crowd of other people from Ironmongers who wanted to know what was going on.

He would never outrun them all. He had to go to ground. His only chance was to try one of the secret routes that led from house to house. There was a network of them, all round Ironmongers. You could slip from one building to another, through attics and cellars and outhouses, without ever coming out into the open air. People used them all the time, to dodge the police or to escape from debt-collectors.

Moulton's cellar was the nearest way into the network.

Charlie plunged down the cellar steps, into the pie shop and winked three times at old Ma Moulton. Then he dived through the rickety door at the far end, before she had time to see that it wasn't the police who were after him.

It was like a warren down there. Six cellars – or was it seven? – were linked together by arches. You could run the whole length of Old Tannery without coming up into the street. Charlie had dodged the police a dozen times like that, and he wasn't the only one.

But it was different trying to dodge Joshua. He wasn't the police. He'd been born by the river, like Charlie, and he knew all the secret routes. All through the cellars, Charlie heard his running feet, just a little way behind, with the rest of the gang following him. And when he reached the last cellar, he could hear Joshua yelling as he scrambled out through the coal hole.

"You wait till I cop hold of you, Charlie Benbow! You'll wish you'd never been born!"

There was no time to think or make a plan. Charlie raced on, diving down any alley that would keep him out of Joshua's way. It was harder in the open streets. The gang spread out, coming at him from two or three directions at once. He had to keep his wits about him to make sure he didn't run into a trap.

Gradually, by instinct almost, he moved

towards the river. He found himself back where the whole thing had started, running along beside the Steps where he had found the brooch. But this time the tide was high against the wall. Deep enough for drowning.

He knew he couldn't run much further. He was staggering and gasping for breath. He tried to keep going, but his foot caught against a stone and he went down hard, banging both knees on the cobbles. Before he could get up again, he heard a loud, triumphant laugh.

In front of him.

Joshua had run round a different way, to cut him off. He was racing out of an alley, not ten yards ahead. When he saw Charlie he stopped running and began to walk steadily towards him, getting his breath back.

Glancing over his shoulder, Charlie saw the rest of the gang behind him, about the same distance away. They were jeering and grinning, because they knew that he was trapped. And they were right. There was no escape this time.

But he was blowed if Joshua was having the brooch! *He* was the one who'd found it! It had stuck in *his* foot! If he couldn't keep it, it was going back in the river!

Dragging himself back on to his feet, Charlie stumbled over to the Steps and lifted his arm, ready to throw the brooch.

Let Joshua mudlark for it if he wanted it so much!

When they saw what he was up to, Joshua and the gang began to run. For a second, as they yelled, Charlie felt a grim delight. He held his arm high, savouring it. Waiting until absolutely the last moment before he tossed the brooch into the water.

The moment didn't come. Before Joshua reached him, there was a new sound. A carriage came clattering on to the cobbles and someone stuck his head out of its window and called to them. It was a gentleman's voice.

"Here a minute, you boys! I want to talk to you!"

4
A Fair Reward

They all froze. Then Joshua leaned forward and tweaked the brooch out of Charlie's hand. Without pausing for a second, he ran towards the carriage, shoving the brooch into his pocket.

Charlie just managed not to shout. He was furious, but he knew it would be stupid to quarrel over the brooch now. The man in the carriage would haul them straight off to the police station if he saw it.

Joshua wasn't going to get away,

though. Charlie followed him up to the carriage, keeping close.

The gentleman leaned out of the window. “Were you boys down here at low tide? Do you know any of the scavengers who look for things in the mud?”

Charlie and Joshua stared at their boots, not answering. Rich men in tall hats usually meant just one thing for boys like them. Trouble.

“Come on, come on!” snapped the gentleman. “It’s a simple question. Do you know anyone who scavenges at low tide?”

“Might do,” Joshua muttered. “Who’s asking?”

The man frowned impatiently. "Don't waste my time, boy. If you know what's good for you, you'll answer my questions. My mother lost something out of a boat last night. It had great sentimental value and there will be a fair reward for anyone who finds it."

From inside the carriage came an old lady's voice. They could see her leaning towards the window as she spoke. "I shall be most grateful to anyone who finds my brooch."

"Brooch?" said Joshua slowly. "It's strange you should say that, ma'am." He slipped a hand into his pocket and pulled out the big, golden brooch. "I was just on my way to the police station with this. To hand it in."

The gentleman gave him a sharp look, but before he could say anything there was a gasp of delight from inside the carriage.

"Is it my brooch? Oh Edwin, it *is* my brooch! The boy has found it! He must be properly rewarded!"

Charlie couldn't believe his ears. "It was me, not him!" he said furiously. "I found it! I was the one!'

But it was no use protesting. Joshua just smirked at him and nodded to the rest of his gang. They all began to shout too, twice as loud as Charlie.

"No it wasn't him that found it, sir, it was me!"

"Me! Me!"

"Me!"

The gentleman waved them away, sighing angrily. "You see, Mother?" he said, over his shoulder. "Boys like this are all liars. There's no hope of helping them."

"Honesty should be rewarded," the old lady said firmly. "These boys have had a bad start in life, but they have seeds of goodness in them. It is our duty to help them."

The gentleman sighed again. "You can't take them all on."

"I realize that. I'm not a fool, Edwin." Suddenly, the old lady sounded very sharp. "The best reward shall be for the boy who handed back the brooch. But you can give each of the others a shilling."

The gentleman did not look happy, but he put his hand into his pocket and found six silver shillings. One for Charlie and one for each member of Joshua's gang. Their hands shot out and he dropped the coins into them without touching them. Then he waved Joshua forward.

"My mother will give you something worth far more than a shilling," he said. "You shall have a chance to better yourself. Come with us now."

With a smug grin at Charlie, Joshua stepped into the carriage and closed the door behind him. Charlie was outraged. Two hours ago, he would have thought himself rich with the shilling he had in his hand. But now he felt cheated.

"It's not fair!" he said. "I was the one

who found the brooch! You know I was, Joshua Vardy!"

Joshua just pulled a face at him, through the window of the coach.

"I–" Charlie would have carried on, but suddenly, behind him, one of the gang sniggered – and he realized what a fool he was to stay there. The moment the carriage drove off, the rest of Joshua's gang would lay into him. And that would mean no reward at all. Not even a shilling. If he wanted to keep that, he had to get away quickly.

The gentleman climbed back into the coach and the coachman picked up the reins. As the horses started to move, Charlie looked round wildly, feeling terribly alone.

But he wasn't alone. Peg and Alfred were running along the river bank towards him. And close behind was Liza, with the little ones panting after her.

Charlie started running to meet them. "Hey!" he yelled. "Come over there, to the coach! You can tell the gentleman –"

But it was too late for that. By the time Charlie reached Peg and Alfred, the coach was already at the corner of the street.

"The brooch..." Charlie panted. "...Joshua had it... the rest of us got a shilling... but Joshua's gone... for the real reward..."

Liza grabbed him by the shoulders and made him stand still. "*Where* has Joshua gone?"

"In that carriage..." Charlie turned to point. They were just in time to see the coach disappear round the corner. Leaning out of the window, waving mockingly at all of them, was a triumphant Joshua.

Charlie bit his lip and looked down at the shilling in his hand.

"Cheer up!" Peg said. "At least you've got that. It'd take you three days to earn a shilling by mudlarking."

"I know," Charlie said gruffly. "But I've still got to go on mudlarking, haven't I? And Joshua..."

Liza put an arm round his shoulders. "What you need is something to cheer you up. Why don't you buy your Ma a big lump of bacon? I'll cook it for her and we can all share the broth tonight. Have a bit of a party. How about that?"

Charlie tried to smile, but he couldn't. He was too choked to speak.

* * *

"Look on the bright side, Charlie," Peg said that evening. "You had the best of it."

They were all in Liza's room, sharing a

fine supper. The bacon was cooked, ready for Charlie to take home, and they were eating the broth it had boiled in – mopping round their bowls with great hunks of bread.

Charlie stared at her. "I did? How d'you make that out?"

"You got a shilling to buy bread and bacon and vegetables.
All I got
was these."

Peg rolled up her sleeves, with a flourish. Her arms were covered in large blue bruises. "When I got back from the river, my sister laid into me good and proper. The bunches weren't made up – and all the flowers were spoiled, in the steam from the washing. There's nothing for me to sell outside the theatre tonight."

"I was in trouble too," Alfred said gloomily. "I got the cane. A dozen of the best for being late to school."

Liza pulled a face. "I got a belting from my dad. He came in before I had a chance to clear all that wet washing off the floor. And you've never heard such a carry-on. I'll bet he's down at the pub now, moaning about me."

"More fool him!" Peg said stoutly. "He doesn't know when he's well off. I wish I got to eat your cooking every day." She reached over to stir the pot and the room was filled with a fine smell of bacon and cabbage, potatoes and onions.

Liza grinned. "Let's eat grand, like Joshua." She dipped into the pot and ladled out a share of the broth for Peg. "Beefsteak pie, madam?"

"Oh no. I'm having poached salmon!" Peg licked her lips. "How about you, young Billy?"

Billy pretended to take a great bite at what was on his spoon. "Lamb cutlets. Big juicy ones."

"Roast pork, with the crackling!" said Charlie.

"Big slices of ham!" said Alfred.

"A great thick pudding with currants!" said Joe. "And cakes and apple pie and – and *ice cream*!"

Sairey-Ann bounced up and down. "Lots of ice cream for me too!"

They went on playing the game while they ate the cabbage and potato. Liza curtsied as she served them out and the others ignored her and talked over her head in loud, high voices, like ladies and gentlemen at a party.

It seemed like part of the joke when Billy suddenly shouted, "There's Joshua!"

"Invite him up for dessert!" Peg said. She waved a hand. "We'll have walnuts and Malaga raisins!"

But Billy didn't laugh. "No – it is him. Look!"

And it was. But what a Joshua! He was slinking in under the arch with no fancy curls, no flash coat and no swagger. His head was shaved, his face was scrubbed clean and he was wearing a short jacket with a collar. Like a little boy.

Peg leaned out of the window. "Made your fortune then, Josh?"

He stopped and looked up at them with a strange expression on his face.

"Too grand for a sup of bacon broth?" said Alfred.

The smell of the bacon was filling the whole court. Joshua drew in a long breath and ran his tongue over his lips. The others stared down at him, wondering what had happened.

"If you come up here, you can have some of the broth," called Liza. To their amazement Joshua made straight for the stairs. Two minutes later, he was sitting by the fire, eating broth as hard as he could go.

"Where's the great reward then?" said Peg, digging him in the ribs. "What did they give you, Josh?"

Joshua looked up from his bowl. "They're going to give me a new start in life!" he said bitterly. "That's what they say. They're round at my Pa's now, getting him to sign some papers. He thinks it's a grand chance for me."

"And is it?" said Liza.

Joshua scowled at her. "What do you think? Look at me! They burnt all my clothes. And shaved off my hair. And gave me a bath – like a baby!"

Sairey-Ann giggled, and he glared at her.

"What about the food?" said Alfred mildly. "Didn't they give you a meal?"

Joshua pulled a terrible face. "Oh, they did that all right! Know what it was? Bread and milk! Said I mustn't eat too rich, till I'd got over being starved."

"Cheek!" said Liza. She spooned some more broth into his bowl. "There's no starving in Ironmongers today. We're having a feast."

Joshua bent over the bowl. He was more interested in eating than talking. But Peg had another question.

"What happens when your Pa's signed the papers?"

"They're going to take me..." Joshua stopped. A crafty look came into his eyes. "Tell you what, young Charlie," he said. "Give me that shilling of yours, and you can have my reward. How about that? I'll tell them it was you that found the brooch."

Charlie wasn't going to fall for that.

"Too late," he said. "The shilling's spent." He stood up. "Fish the bacon out of the pot, Liza, and I'll take it home to Ma."

Liza hooked it out and dropped it into a dish. "Here you are. Hope your ma enjoys it."

"She will," Charlie said. "It's weeks since we had any bacon." He covered the dish with a plate and carried it to the door. Then he paused, looking over his shoulder at Joshua. "You might as well tell me," he said casually. "What is this new start they're giving you?"

Joshua shuddered. "They're giving me a job. At their house in the country. Me! The flash king of the mudlarks!"

"What's wrong with the country?" said Liza. "Some folks like it."

Joshua pulled a face. "There's nothing there but mud."

"That ought to suit you," Charlie said. "If you're the king of the mudlarks."

"River mud's different," Joshua growled. "That's full of treasures – things you can sell. But country mud's got nothing except cows and sheep. And *pigs*. Did you ever smell a pig?"

"Is that the job?" said Alfred. "Working on a farm?"

Joshua avoided his eyes. "No, it's – more of an indoor job."

"Footman?" said Liza. "Valet? Butler's apprentice?"

"Not exactly." Slowly, Joshua's face was turning pink.

Peg grinned. "You might as well spit it out. Your dad's sure to tell everyone anyway."

Joshua looked down at his boots. "They

say – I can help the cook and run her errands. To start with."

Peg burst out laughing. "No need to fret about the mud, then." She patted his arm. "You won't be getting outside much. There'll be too much to do in the kitchen. Heaps of dirty dishes to wash."

"Potatoes to peel," said Liza.

"Knives to sharpen," said Alfred.

"Greasy pans to scour," said Charlie.

"You'll be up before dawn…"

"And working till midnight…"

"And…"

But Joshua wasn't waiting to hear any more. He jumped to his feet and backed out of the room. They heard him running down the stairs as fast as he could go.

Charlie went to the window and looked out. There were a couple of footmen in uniform, waiting in the court. When Joshua emerged, they each took one of his arms and started to lead him off.

Putting the bacon dish on the window

sill, Charlie opened the window and leaned out. "Hey, Joshua!" he called.

Joshua looked up and Charlie waved cheerfully.

"Thank you for saving me! I'd rather be a mudlark than wash dishes!"

Joshua shook his fist and Charlie chuckled and shut the window. When he turned round, all the others were laughing at him.

"Still angry about losing the reward ?" said Liza.

"Still wish you'd hung on to the brooch?" said Peg.

Charlie shook his head. "I've got all the reward I want," he said.

Joe looked at him solemnly, his eyes

wide. “I’m glad those men didn’t take you away. You’ve got to take me and Sairey-Ann down to the river.”

“And me!” Billy said fiercely. “We’ve got to find Liza a new stick for stirring the washing.”

“Right!” said Charlie. “We’ll do that tomorrow!”

He grinned at them all. Then he ran off, down the stairs and across the court to his mother. Bringing home the bacon.

About the author

I've always wanted to know what it would be like to be someone else. That's why I write stories.

I wrote *The Treasure in the Mud* because I wanted to know how it would feel to be a boy like Charlie, living in London a hundred and fifty years ago. I found out about his life by reading books, especially one called *London Labour and the London Poor* by Henry Mayhew. Then I pretended to *be* Charlie – and the story came.

It would have been quite a different story, of course, if I'd been pretending to be Peg or Liza or Joshua...